Have You Seen This?

तुम्ही हे पाहिलंत का?

TEXT *Arthi Anand Navaneeth*
PICTURES *Roomani Kulkarni*
TRANSLATION *Suneeti Jain*

लेखन आरती आनंद नवनीत
चित्रे रूमानी कुलकर्णी
अनुवाद सुनीति जैन

Tulika

Have you seen a boat that walks?

तुम्ही बोट पाहिली आहे जी चालते?

A house that spins?

घर जे गरागरा फिरतं?

A chair that jumps?

खुर्ची जी उडी मारते?

A door that runs?

दरवाजा जो धावतो?

Have you seen a flower that talks?

तुम्ही फूल पाहिलं आहे जे बोलते?

A balloon that laughs?

फुगा जो हसतो?

A giraffe that swims?

जिराफ जो पोहतो?

A tree that flies?

झाड जे उडतं?

Have you seen a crow that cooks?

तुम्ही कावळा पाहिला आहे जो स्वयंपाक करतो?

An auto that eats?

ऑटोरिक्शा जी खाते?

A star that sings?

चांदणी जी गाते?

A cloud that yawns?

ढग जो जांभया देतो?

Have you seen a book that reads?

तुम्ही पुस्तक पाहिलं आहे जे वाचतं?

A clock that sleeps?

घड्याळ जे झोपतं?

A bed that snores?

अंथरूण जे घोरतं?

A phone that dreams?

फोन जो स्वप्न पाहतो?

A cat that crows?

मांजर जी आरवते?

KOKARAKOOOO!
कुकूचकू!

Have you seen this? / Tumhi hai pahilat ka? (English-Marathi)

ISBN 978-93-5046-195-2

First published in India, 2012

Originally in English

Published by
Tulika Publishers, 24/1 Ganapathy Colony Third Street, Teynampet, Chennai 600 018, India
email tulikabooks@vsnl.com *website* www.tulikabooks.com

Printed and bound by
Lokavani Southern Printers Pvt. Ltd, 122 Greams Road, Chennai 600 006, India